How to
STAY POSITIVE
without
LOSING YOUR
MIND!

C. S. Jordan

CONTENTS

Foreword

Having gone through depression, I've learned a few things: You don't get sympathy points from the Universe for being sad — justifiably or not and the Universe has no feelings. I use the Universe to refer to the world within the "real" world we live in — the bubble God has created for us that surrounds us. It is an unseen world that responds to your thoughts and emotions and for better or worse, affects your daily life.

This book does not offer medical advice or professional therapy, but practical advice to harness the power of positivity, reduce stress, and transform your life.

"Positivity is the key to happiness, the key to positivity is action"

CHAPTER 1

YOUR UNIVERSE

The Universe is like a giant, impersonal machine. It operates according to its own rules and set purpose. *Your* Universe is a living breathing entity within the greater Universe. It revolves around you. Not your spouse, your children, your parents, your best friends, but you and only you. It is responsive to your thoughts and feelings and is always at your command and, like any well-built machine, its output is a direct result of what you put in. It feeds off your thoughts, feelings, perceptions and presumptions and uses them to create the real world you live in.

You can liken the process to using a Geiger counter. But instead of detecting radiation, and the signal getting stronger as it gets closer to the source, it has been calibrated to detect negativity or positivity within *you* and react accordingly.

Once either is detected it becomes a perpetual generating machine, generating negative or positive experiences proportionate to the level found within the source (*you*). Therefore negativity begets negativity, positivity begets positivity, until the connection to the source is broken.

Now it may seem like every little negative thought you think, every fleeting negative emotion you feel can send your world spiraling downhill, but DO NOT BE AFRAID, this is actually a good thing.

You now know the rules of the game and when you know the rules of a game you have a real chance at winning. You now have a tool that you can use to achieve some semblance of control when life seems to be operating at random.

Now how do you maintain a positive mindset when everything in your life seems to be working against you?

How do you attract the things you want into your life and less of the things you don't? Why is it necessary for you to maintain a positive outlook anyway? How can you stay positive without losing your mind? Well, let's get into it.

THOUGHTS:

_____

_____

_____

_____

_____

_____

_____

_____

_____

_____

_____

_____

_____

_____

_____

_____

_____

_____

_____

_____

_____

_____

_____

_____

_____

_____

_____

_____

_____

_____

_____

_____

"Approach every day with the confident expectation of positive outcomes"

CHAPTER 2

BEING POSITIVE IS NOT THE SAME AS BEING HAPPY

First of all, let's establish that there is a difference between being positive and being happy. Many people confuse the two. That's where the problem begins. If you believe the solution to your problems is that you just need to be happy, no matter what, and go about pursuing that path, you have set yourself a daunting task that will be met with much psychological resistance. You've set a high bar that will be difficult to maintain.

While positivity can lead to happiness, happiness and positivity are not the same. Happiness can be best described as a destination. While on the journey to that destination there are many hills and valleys. At any point along the journey, you can experience the feeling of satisfaction and contentment. So, like an oasis in the desert, you can arrive at your destination (*happiness*) at any point along the journey.

Positivity is a state of mind in which you rest your thoughts and emotional well-being with confidence in the hope and expectation of good things to come. In effect, positivity is the car in which your journey is being taken in. As long as you maintain your car in good condition and keep it filled with gas, you will reach your destination.

So, does positivity mean walking around with a permasmile on your face or suppressing very real feelings of hurt, anxiety and even despair? Absolutely not.

You may have been conditioned to believe that if you can just learn to act happy, a positive 'state of being' will naturally follow. Basically, 'fake it 'til you make it.' That is not the case and, as you will soon learn, you can not fool the Universe.

While you need to have a positive outlook on life in order to be happy, you do not need to be happy to maintain a positive outlook. Happiness is fleeting, and, because life happens, it is not healthy to base your emotional well-being on something ephemeral.

Therefore positivity is the key to happiness, but the key to positivity is *action*.

Positivity is something you *do* on a daily basis. And if you do it, you will see positive effects. Positivity is not a fleeting emotion. It is something that you must make an integral part of your life. Every day, you will make the conscious decision to approach your life with the confident expectation of positive outcomes. This is your first step on your road to happiness.

You may find it difficult to stay positive. It is not easy to maintain a positive outlook when you are in pain (emotional or physical).

It can be tempting to focus on your pain and to believe there is no hope. It may be easier to give up on the idea of being happy altogether. But you are never alone, and you should never give up on your happiness.

THOUGHTS:

_____

_____

_____

_____

_____

_____

_____

_____

_____

_____

_____

_____

_____

_____

_____

"On the road trip of life, plan your rest stops"

CHAPTER 3

POSITIVITY IS A STRUGGLE

Are you trying to find ways to be more positive but it is just not working?

If you have been struggling with depression, anxiety, or any other mental health condition, you might find it difficult to be positive. You might find it difficult to see the good in your life or even the good in yourself, no matter how hard you try.

When you are feeling this way, STOP and look within.

Assess how negative your thoughts are. You hold on to these negative thoughts and feelings for a reason. Like a loose thread that you pull and the fabric comes apart, this negativity may, in fact, be holding you together. It has formed the foundation of how you view the world and without it, you may feel lost.

Your thoughts are like a perpetual motion machine in which you can insert a new directive to change course at any time, but it never stops affecting your life.

Assess the level of resentment, blame or guilt you have stored inside you. Assess whether these thoughts and feelings are directed towards a specific person or event in your life.

Like drinking buddies to an alcoholic, this negativity has enabled your misery.

If you want to move forward, you will have to leave these thoughts and feelings behind.

You may have to reach out a little farther away from your comfort zone to reach a lifeline. When you reach it hold on and don't let go.

You are not alone. Even if you believe that the whole world is against you and no one is on your side, there is support to be found if you seek it out. Many people have found themselves in your very same situation. What you see from the outside are the results of the different choices they have made, for better or worse.

Positivity is a struggle for many people.

Think of it like trying to hold a door open on a windy day, just when you think you have it propped open another gust of wind comes along to shut it again.

While focusing on the positive in your life will make you feel better and more confident, if you find yourself struggling, try approaching it from a different angle.

Remember, positivity is not happiness.

Instead of trying to force yourself into a positive state of mind, shift your focus onto the things that bring you joy and build from there. There are many ways you can bring more positivity into your daily life, but they require a commitment to the process.

One way that is often helpful is taking on a new habit. For example, if you want to cultivate a more positive outlook on your life, try meditation. Meditation is an ancient practice that has been shown to improve concentration and can improve the quality of your life in a variety of ways. It is very easy to incorporate this practice into your life. You can meditate sitting on a cushion, lying on your bed, or even just focusing your mind on your breathing at different times throughout the day. There are many types of meditations, the one you choose is up to you.

Another way to develop your positivity muscles is to incorporate affirmations into your daily routine. Affirmations are statements that you make to yourself that are positive, encouraging or goal-oriented. Repeat them softly and with positive intention. They can be as short as a sentence or paragraph or just one word.

Affirmations can be a powerful tool to adjust your mindset and help you accomplish the things you want. The most important thing is to pick affirmations that are positive and uplifting. Your affirmations should make you feel good and remind you of your life purpose or immediate goals.

Always strive to be as positive as possible and use encouraging words when you talk to yourself. The language you use when you talk to yourself resonates longer and louder than anything spoken to you by others and often tends to repeat in a continuous loop in your mind like that tune you can't get out of your head.

It can be as simple as saying affirmations to yourself at bedtime, just when you're feeling drowsy. When you reach a state of deep sleep, your subconscious mind is much more receptive to new messages. You can say affirmations as part of your nighttime routine or, if you're more of a morning person, you can say them as soon as you wake up.

Still another way to cultivate positivity is to focus on the present moment and try not to worry too much about the future. If you are doing everything that needs to be done now, can the future help but fall in line? When you're having a tough time, change your perspective.

When it seems like everything you touch is doomed to fail, change your perspective on the situation. Negative thoughts will only make things worse and lead you to feel defeated. But when you change your perspective, the outcome may turn out to be more advantages than you imagined.

Sometimes, not getting what you want may be the best possible outcome.

The key difference between approaching life through a positive filter or a negative filter is clarity. Through a positive filter, you can see clearly what is happening. You can think practically. You can practically weigh your options. Your vision is clear, your mind is clear. Through a negative filter, everything is a fog. Nothing makes sense. Your mind is confused and you can't think clearly. Can you really expect yourself to make rational decisions in this condition?

If you consider yourself a news junkie or even a casual consumer of hard news, it can be hard to stay positive when we have so many negative things happening in the world. When you're getting bombarded with negativity on a daily basis, it becomes increasingly difficult to see the brighter side of things. The more negativity you see, the more negativity will seep into your mind.

It becomes a vicious cycle that is difficult to break out of.

It's easy to get caught up in the problems of the world. There are so many things happening that make us feel like we have no control or that we can't do anything to help. But, there are plenty of ways that we can still find happiness and joy in our lives — even when everything around us seems bleak.

You are not responsible for the world. You can not control the world. You already have your hands full. The best way to find positivity is by focusing on what you can control rather than what you can not. The moment you stop trying to control every aspect of your life, especially where others are concerned, positivity will start to increase in your life.

You may be struggling to keep your thoughts and emotions from drifting towards negativity and doubt. Start now by incorporating a positive mindset into your daily life. It is not an easy task when you have had a lifetime of conditioning towards a

21

negative thought cycle. With the help of these fifteen steps, you can guide yourself towards a positive mindset and start living your life to its fullest.

1. Find your purpose. If your life is only about working and paying bills, you have a problem. The key to happiness is finding your purpose in life and finding fulfillment through it. When you focus on what makes you feel fulfilled, your sense of purpose will reveal itself and your happiness will skyrocket.

2. Put positive people in your life. Positive people make for positive experiences. Both positivity and negativity are contagious, so choose your associates wisely.

3. Use affirmations. Affirmations encourage positive thoughts and can be applied to any aspect of your life.

4. Control what you can, release the rest. When you try too hard to control everything around you, it won't be long before things start to spiral out of control.

5. Find a hobby. As the saying goes, 'an idle mind is the devil's playground.' Discover something new or indulge in something you love. Give yourself less time to dwell on negativity. Hobbies are also a great way to express your creativity and get away from the stresses of modern life. Whether it's playing guitar or painting, there's something out there for everyone.

6. Exercise. Exercise releases endorphins in your brain, instantly elevates your mood and gives you energy, which, in turn, will make you feel better about yourself and life in general. It also leads to weight

loss which will give you even more energy and make you look your best!

7. Eat healthy. Eating healthy foods will help you lose weight and keep your mind and body functioning properly. Eating junk food will cause you to gain weight, feel sluggish and less energetic.

8. Socialize. Spending time with friends or family can reduce stress levels, which will make you feel centered and restful. This only applies if you're a social animal some people enjoy being on their own.

9. Unsocialize. If you're the type who likes spending time alone, then do so. If being around people causes you *more* stress, then carve out some

alone time for yourself to do the things you enjoy or just relax.

10. Drink lots of water. Dehydration can cause fatigue and even sluggishness, so drinking water will help keep your body replenished. You will notice the difference particularly if tend to drink more juice or soda than water.

11. Get enough sleep. Not everyone needs 8 hours of sleep, you must determine how much is right for you. Regardless, waking up refreshed after a full, undisturbed sleep will reduce stress levels, which, in turn, will increase your energy level throughout the day.

12. Slow down on alcohol and caffeine. Alcohol and caffeine can increase anxiety, making you feel more tired. Limiting their intake, avoiding them

altogether, or relegating them to certain times of the day or week, will help you sleep better and have more energy throughout the day. Also, the less time spent recovering from the effects of alcohol, the more time you can spend getting things done.

13. Take a break. Constantly overworking yourself will cause your performance to *decrease*, as well as feelings of fatigue and burnout. You will be working, but getting less useful work done. Taking a break once in a while will allow your mind and body to replenish themselves so that you can come back strong!

14. Meditate. If you're looking for a quick ten minutes to clear your mind, meditation is a great option. It will help you achieve a state of peace and relaxation that will allow

your creativity to flow, stress levels to drop and restful sleep to occur.

15. Keep a Diary or Journal. Keeping a journal can help you keep track of your dreams and goals. It can also help reduce stress and anxiety by assisting you in downloading your day and getting things off your chest you may be struggling with.

THOUGHTS:

_____

_____

_____

_____

_____

_____

_____

_____

_____

_____

_____

_____

_____

_____

_____

Positivity Is a Struggle

_____

_____

_____

_____

_____

_____

_____

_____

_____

_____

_____

_____

_____

_____

_____

_____

"Negativity shared is negativity doubled"

CHAPTER 4

NEGATIVITY IS A COMFY COUCH

Negativity is a comfy couch with all the familiar lumps and bumps, carefully molded to the contours of your body from years of use. From the moment you settle in, it lulls you to sleep. It is a lumpy, bumpy, comfy couch that you have to force yourself out of, push yourself up from. While it may not provide a restful sleep, it is comfortable and familiar. You'll find that when you want to escape from it, it is hard to climb out of, but you must, as settling in will come in direct conflict with your goals and aspirations.

Negativity can spread like a virus. And, like any virus, it can be persistent and invasive. It can make you believe that you are not worthy of achieving your dreams, that you are not good enough, that life is not worth living, that you are not loved.

It can also spread quickly from one person to another.

When you feel yourself spreading negativity, it's important to take a step back and refocus on the positive.

The internet is a place where people feel they can be themselves, for better or worse. They can download whatever is on their minds and share their opinions on any topic. This has enabled the world to see the good and bad sides of humanity.

With social media being such a large platform, it is easy for you to share your negative thoughts and engage in cynical banter with people you don't even know. It is even easier for you to receive validation from others who agree with your cynical take on the topic of the day. However, negativity shared is negativity doubled. After the temporary high of having your opinions shared or thumbed up, nothing productive has been advanced, and it does not make you feel good. It does not make anyone feel good. This does not mean you don't acknowledge the problems in the world but instead focus on what you can do about them from where you are. If you can see the problem, you may be the right person to find the solution.

Anxiety, worry, self-doubt, depression, and so on. These are all forms of negative thinking. You may not always know where it comes from or how it creeps in, but you do know it is exhausting, debilitating, and can destroy your present and your future.

Spend too much time focusing on the negative things in your life, you will start to feel overwhelmed and even powerless. When you feel overwhelmed or powerless it may feel like the only thing you can do is complain — about your job, your family, your life, the state of the world. But it is not your only option.

What can you do to get out of that lumpy, bumpy couch and into a positive and productive life?

1. As soon as you recognize it, stop negativity in its tracks and commit to not spreading it to others.

2. Try to avoid social media, or other sources of negativity, for a few hours each day.

3. At work, do not gossip with your co-workers or talk about your personal problems with others who have no insight or power to resolve them.

4. When you're out and about, something as simple as complaining about the weather can trigger a cascade of negative thoughts and conversations.

5. Accept responsibility for your future. You are the one in charge of

your life. Don't blame others for the problems you're experiencing. *Your* actions will determine how your future will turn out.

6. Give yourself a break. Negative thinking is usually a symptom of a bigger problem. It may be that you are feeling overwhelmed, anxious, or stressed. If this is the case, give yourself a break and spend time doing things you enjoy.

7. Stop and breathe. When you are feeling overwhelmed, take a few moments to stop, breathe and recenter yourself. This is a great way to stop stress from creeping up on you and to relax.

8. When you're feeling discouraged, make a list of all the good things that are happening in your life right now and read it every day. You may

surprise yourself with the good things you've allowed to go unacknowledged.

Negativity may be your default setting. Why? Because it's easy. Most people have been conditioned to turn to the cynical or sarcastic when faced with challenges in their lives, so when things start to go sideways, you easily default to your 'go-to'. It is also a buffer. No one wants to get hurt. If you sense circumstances may not end up going your way, you are more likely to place a cushion around your feelings and expectations. 'I didn't want that job anyway' or 'I knew that was going to happen' or 'It figures.' Unfortunately, these 'buffers' have a surreptitious effect on your life. When you consistently hold the thought of something bad happening, it does happen. You need to be open to seeing things for what they are, with no negative connotations or expectations about them.

Negative attitudes are not always bad. They can be a way to cope with difficult situations.

There is no denying that negativity has its drawbacks. However, it also has its benefits. It can be a way for you to make sense of the world around you. It can also be satisfying. Really. When your day starts to go south, the feeling of 'I knew it' or 'I told you so' actually brings a form of comfort. Being 'right' fosters a sense of stability. There is unsettling comfort in poorly met expectations; nothing lost, nothing gained. If you don't get that job, you won't have to meet and interact with a whole new group of people or leave your comfort zone. It would probably have never worked out anyway.

When you believe something was going to happen a certain way and your expectations are confirmed, it is ironically *satisfying*.

What is being created is a negative cycle that can lead to more bad things happening to you. Your Universe responds quickly and will set events in motion as you 'will' it, often before you are consciously aware they are happening. While you can subconsciously slip into a negative state of mind, it remains your choice to stay there.

When you encounter a negative thought, it is important to immediately identify it and stop it in its tracks. Do not give it time to settle in and get comfortable. When you consistently hold the thought of something bad happening, it happens.

Change can only happen when you realize that you will need to alter the way you think and process information in order to cultivate a positive outlook and find happiness. It takes effort to change this way of thinking and you must be consistent.

It's important to remember that positivity is not something that you can just turn on and off. To produce positive effects in your life, your positivity switch must always be turned on.

The key is to change your default setting from negativity to positivity.

There is evil in the world and you have to know that. Positivity isn't about wiping out evil or pretending it doesn't exist. But there is also good and you must align yourself with it:

1. Think about the people who have been good to you, you will realize that there are so many people who are good to others as well.

2. Focus on what you can do, not what you can't.

3. Don't let fear control your life, but instead challenge it and see it as a chance to grow.

4. Think about what you can do today that will make the world a better place for someone else.

Stop thinking about what is wrong with the world and be a part of making it right.

THOUGHTS:

_____

_____

_____

_____

_____

_____

_____

_____

_____

_____

_____

_____

_____

_____

_____

_____

_____

_____

_____

_____

_____

_____

_____

_____

_____

_____

_____

_____

_____

_____

_____

_____

"If everyone in the world is against you, you must always be on your side"

CHAPTER 5

WHY YOU MUST STAY POSITIVE

You must strive to stay positive if you want your life trajectory to reach the heights of success or at least have half a chance. We live in a world where negativity is in abundance. Many things in life can negatively affect you. If you are like most people, you have a lot of things to worry about. You have your work, your kids, your health, and your finances to worry about. You never know what is going to happen next and there is a lot of stress in your life.

You have certainly had days where you've felt down and out. You may even have had days when you feel like you want to give up. When you find yourself in a negative state, it's important to find a way to get yourself out of it. There's an old saying, 'Where the mind goes, the body will follow.' In fact, where your mind goes, your life will follow, obediently. There is no easy way to say this but it is true, you have to stay positive. Here's why.

Have you ever felt like nothing is going right? From the moment you wake up your day seems to spiral from bad to worse? Well, you're right. It is not a figment of your imagination. However, from the moment you notice things starting to go off the rails; the microwave stops working, the traffic jam is going to make you late for your appointment, your new phone crashes to the ground and the screen breaks — even though the phone case you just bought said that would never happen — you must grasp the opportunity to turn things around.

These are defining moments. What you do next will decide whether or not your day is going to go into freefall or rise from the ashes. When things start going downhill, just stop. (*Obviously, not in the middle of traffic*). Stop what you're doing. Pull over. Breathe.

Why? You need to break the connection. Negative experiences yield negative thoughts. Every negative thought, every negative emotion, is a link in a chain. The more negative experiences you allow to be strung together without stopping creates more links in the chain. The trick is to not allow the chain to get long enough and strong enough to pull you down.

Negativity will also cause your body to produce a lot of stress hormones which can lead to health problems like chronic fatigue, insomnia, and weight gain.

Whatever is going on in your life, if you think it can't get worse, you're wrong. I'm sure there are many elements in your life (some of which you can probably put a first and last name to) that you feel are working overtime to make bad things happen. If you are going to succeed, you must find a strategy to overcome these negative elements no matter the circumstance.

THOUGHTS:

_____

_____

_____

_____

_____

_____

_____

_____

_____

_____

_____

_____

_____

_____

_____

_____

_____

_____

_____

_____

_____

_____

_____

_____

_____

_____

_____

_____

_____

_____

_____

_____

"Positivity is like a muscle, the more you exercise it, the stronger it becomes"

CHAPTER 6

YOU CAN'T FOOL THE UNIVERSE

The mind is a powerful thing. Along with your thoughts and emotions, it works in conjunction with your Universe to create and control the world you know.

It receives its instructions, creates a blueprint, and goes to work orchestrating your life according to that plan.

Your Universe is always providing what you ask for. Even as you follow your designated course, a course that is a direct line to your destination; your doubts, lack of confidence, change of mind, or even wavering between various options, can make the difference between whether you arrive at your destination or completely veer off course towards another endpoint. Remain rudderless or goalless for too long and you may find yourself going in circles.

So, therefore, once you know what you want, you can not be of two minds about it. Your Universe is not your best friend to which you can chit-chat about the possible outcomes of every random thought that pops into your head.

For example, let's say you want to be a teacher in a foreign country and you've told all your friends that you're going to be a teacher in a foreign country and you have been screening schools and locations for months. Then all of a sudden, the idea of becoming a teacher at home starts to resonate with you. You start exploring the possibility of local school systems and locations.

Your thoughts of teaching internationally have now been taken over by teaching domestically. Now you start applying for domestic teaching jobs. You also start applying for international teaching positions just to hedge your bets. One of three things is likely to occur. You may get many interviews for international teaching positions. You may get an interview for a domestic teaching position. Or you may get no interviews for either. Now let's explore why.

1. You may get many interviews for international teaching positions. You've had a longer period of time to be excited about teaching internationally, to desire it and establish confidently that it is what you want, therefore it has had a longer period of time to settle in your heart. The universe has already mapped out your destination and a detailed plan to get you there.

2. You may get one or two interviews for teaching domestically. Teaching domestically has captured your heart and mind. But while it has excited you, it has not had time to capture your full attention. You

have not completely let go of the idea of teaching internationally. You have even told your friends you will be teaching internationally. So, in the back of your mind, you still feel a responsibility for declaring your previous intentions (*i.e.*, will they still think it's cool if I get a domestic teaching job?). Therefore, your Universe is still unclear as to which direction you truly want to go, but it has enough information to start you on your journey.

3. You may get no interviews for either. As your desire to teach is connected to where you'll be teaching, your Universe is completely confused. It doesn't know what you want, so it can not design the road map to get you there.

That is not to say you can not change your mind. However, if you change your mind, change it resolutely.

You may have heard the term 'ask for what you want.' When it comes to your Universe, you don't have to ask for what you want, you need to *know* what you want and be of one mind about it. No doubt. No confusion. No wavering back and forth. Make sure you come to a determined mind after researching, comparing, exploring your opportunities and alternatives, and *then* make your final decision. Once your decision is made, be resolute about it, take the necessary actions, then wait with positive expectancy and allow your Universe to bring it to you.

You do not communicate with your Universe with words. You communicate with your heart and soul and mind. This is why you can't fool your Universe. Regardless of what you say to others and tell yourself, it knows what you truly feel and what you actually believe.

THOUGHTS:

_____

_____

_____

_____

_____

_____

_____

_____

_____

_____

_____

_____

_____

_____

_____

_____

_____

_____

_____

_____

_____

_____

_____

_____

_____

_____

_____

_____

_____

_____

_____

"The more you practice positive behavior, the easier to let go of negative ones"

CHAPTER 7

TREAT YOURSELF BETTER

Change your behaviors and habits. The more you practice positive behaviors, the easier it will be to let go of your negative ones. However, you don't have to jump into the deep end of the pool to accomplish this.

For example, if you want to stop smoking, decide that you are going to go without cigarettes for one day a week. This is a lot easier than quitting cold turkey. If you are constantly late for work or other appointments, alter your work and appointment times to 30 minutes before the actual start time. In other words, your noon appointments are now 11:30 am appointments. If you want to start eating healthier, it will be easier to stop eating unhealthy foods than it will be to start eating healthy foods. A commitment to avoid unhealthy foods leaves only healthier alternatives.

Habits are part of your coping mechanism. Coping mechanisms are ways of dealing with stress and anxiety. Therefore, it's a lot easier to incorporate a new positive habit than to stop a negative one. You will now train your mind to do different *actions* when stress and anxiety are triggered allowing you to slowly let go of negative ones.

Be patient with yourself. You want to see results and you want to see them now. So when you are not getting the results you want, it is easy to get frustrated and give up. Focus solely on creating your new behavior and not the end result. The results will come in their own time. Your objective is to create new habits and it takes time for your new positive habits to take effect. Patience is key!

Guard your self-talk. It is not only your behavior that affects your progress. You should be aware of the thoughts you hold about yourself and the things you say to yourself.

Self-talk is a big part of your life. If you want to make a positive change in your life, then you need to start with your self-talk. These also include the beliefs and images you hold in your mind about who you are, what you look like and how you believe others perceive you. Never underestimate your mind's ability to hold a completely erroneous view of how you are perceived by others.

You may be prone to negative self-talk. Once it becomes a habit, it takes a conscious, deliberate effort to stop. Negative self-talk can destroy your self-confidence and make you question your abilities.

If you have weaned yourself away from negative self-talk, you still need to be on your guard. It usually creeps in when everything seems to be going well and then something unexpected happens or something you thought was under control begins to fall apart.

Maybe you have been working out religiously and completely revised your diet only to discover that you've *gained* weight or you have been searching for a job longer than you expected or you are experiencing a breakup, stay vigilant.

Don't turn on yourself and become your own enemy. If everyone in the world is against you, you must always be on your side.

Stop. Breathe. Recenter yourself. Remember, not getting what you want may lead to a better outcome.

You may discover a more sustainable diet program that can comfortably help you reach your goal, you may find a job in an unexpected field that is more in line with your personal ambitions and you may meet the love of your life.

Write down your thoughts about yourself, then replace any negative inferences with positive ones. Focus on your positive traits, what makes you unique and the things you enjoy. You'll be amazed at how much more motivated you will feel when you start thinking positively about yourself.

THOUGHTS:

_____

_____

_____

_____

_____

_____

_____

_____

_____

_____

_____

_____

_____

_____

_____

_____

_____

_____

_____

_____

_____

_____

_____

_____

_____

_____

_____

_____

_____

_____

_____

_____

_____

"Let go and let God"

CHAPTER 8

LET IT GO

Let go of what you can't control and take control of yourself, your thoughts, your focus, your safety and your well-being.

At times it can be hard to keep up with the ever-changing world around you. When you are stressed and overwhelmed, it's easy to lose sight of what's important.

Take control of your thoughts and focus on what you can control rather than what you cannot. When you feel like you are drowning in a sea of chaos, step back and take a deep breath.

It's easy to get caught up in your day-to-day life and start to feel as if you're tied to a treadmill and you can't get off. It can be hard to keep up with everything, and it's easy to feel overwhelmed by the things that we have to do. However, you don't have to feel this way. It's important to remember that you are not in control of everything that happens in your life, but you are in control of how you react to it. You can't control other people, but you can control your reactions to their behavior. It's important to take care of yourself and make sure that you don't let the things that happen in your life overwhelm you.

When you assume control and take responsibility, you will feel in charge and less a victim of life's circumstances. You will no longer feel helpless and hopeless. Like a parent that has more control of his life than a child, suddenly, you can take advantage of the host of options available to you.

Have you ever found yourself in a situation where you are so angry, resentful or regretful that you feel like you're about to explode or implode? Sometimes, you don't know what to do with your feelings and you end up hating the person or event that is triggering you. Part of the process of healing from these incidents or encounters is to release the energy you've given to these negative triggers.

It is never about changing the other person but rather finding your own peace.

Everyone you meet has their own life story, life plan, and good or bad intentions towards the world, all of which may have absolutely nothing to do with you.

Letting go doesn't mean you have to forget the person or situation. It means you have a choice to make: move forward and put the past in the past, or dwell in resentment and negativity.

Life moves in one direction. You can't change the past. Let's say you've been cheated or robbed and to this day it's a continuing thorn in your side. There is not a day that goes by that you don't think of it and experience all the negative emotions that come up as a result. You may even fashion elaborate scenarios of what you would have done or could have done, but did not do at that time. Knowing you can't change the past, what do you do? What are your options?

For the sake of your mental health, you will need to let it go.

Outside of helping the authorities catch and prosecute the bad guys, you will need to let it go.

The positive is that by helping to catch the thieves, you're potentially saving lives, and preventing future victims. You may even want to take a self-defense class or carry protection to restore your confidence and be prepared in case you find yourself in a similar situation. All positive things.

The negative is continuing to think about it outside of anything else you can realistically do. Reliving the incident again and again in your mind, including all the alternative scenarios, is not helpful.

Anything outside of what you can actually do *now*, in the present, will result in negativity, anger and resentment, all of which will continue to hurt you long after this incident has passed.

As you attempt to place this incident in perspective and positively move forward with your life, you may find it strange that your mind won't let it go as easily as you would like. To your mind, it will feel strange that you're not thinking about it every day. It will feel like you're letting the crooks off the hook. This is righteous negativity. You believe you have a right to be angry and subsequently, you should be holding on to the memory and all the indignation that comes with it. Your Universe has no ability to process these types of nuances. Negativity produces more negativity.

Once again, you have a choice to make. You can move forward implementing the positive actions that you can take, real efforts that can have a positive impact on the situation, or negatively impact your present and future by wallowing in resentment and anger.

You may have been told that you need to forgive and forget.   Realistically, you don't have to forgive anyone.   You don't have to forget anything.   But you do need to move forward and do so without bitterness and resentment.

This point can not be stressed enough. Whatever form of negativity you allow a place in your mind and heart, regardless of its source or its righteousness, will have a negative effect on your life.

Letting go is about releasing the resentments of the past to focus on the possibilities of the future.

Do you believe you have the power to make someone who has hurt you unhurt you? Do you believe allowing yourself to sink into hopelessness and despair will help them understand how much they have hurt you? The greater the pain, hurt, resentment and anger that is present in your mind, heart and soul, the greater the effect it will have on *you*.

It is important to emphasize, once again, that holding a positive state of mind is not about happiness. It *is* about clarity; being able to make rational decisions with a clear, unbiased mind and allowing your Universe to map your bright, new future.

Hate. Resentment. Regret. Jealousy. Let it go. All of it. The messier your life is, the more you need to let go. There is no more room for it. You have no more time to give to it. You are now on a new path.

THOUGHTS:

_____

_____

_____

_____

_____

_____

_____

_____

_____

_____

_____

_____

_____

_____

_____

"You are never alone"

CHAPTER 9

GRIEF AND BURNOUT

Grief is a natural part of life, but it can be debilitating. Whether it's the death of a loved one, a breakup, or a job loss, you may experience moments in your life when you feel like you are going to crumble. Whatever it may be, there are ways to get through difficult times without having to feel overwhelmed.

Your mind and body can become very vulnerable at these times, leaving you feeling exhausted and unsure of what to do next. There is no right way to deal with grief.

You may want to talk about your feelings and find talking to friends and family helpful or to download your thoughts into a journal or you may prefer to be alone and want to isolate yourself from the world in search of peace.

Take up a new activity or hobby to distract your mind or take a break from work and social media. Find a way that works best for you. There are no right or wrong answers.

Everyone experiences some form of grief in their life. When experiencing grief, you will need to take care of yourself and keep yourself healthy, so you will have the strength to overcome it. While you may feel disengaged and overwhelmed, you have not been given a pass to indulge in self-destructive behavior. Whether it be drinking, drugs, overeating, driving under the influence or with excessive speed, you should have enough respect for your loved one to not use their death as an excuse to engage in behavior that could harm yourself or others, physically or emotionally.

Be honest with yourself about what you are feeling. Stepping back allows you to be able to grieve, reflect and heal.

As grief can sometimes lead to feelings of self-blame and guilt which can lead to depression, it is important to preserve your mental health.

Many times when people lose someone special in their life, their strongest desire is to join them. The pain of their loss is so palpable that they become consumed by such thoughts. If you have lost a loved one — a child, a close friend, a family member or the love of your life, know this, they do not need you. No matter how they left this world, they do not need your comfort, your companionship, your protection or your presence. They are now in the hands of God and need absolutely nothing from you, except the one thing they wanted for you in life, your happiness. Gift them that happiness.

Grieve the loss of their presence in your life. But remember, you are the reason they joined the military, worked two jobs, reorganized their life to make a comfortable place for you, got up every day, smiled so easily, and even made provisions for you for the day when they could no longer be a part of your life.

After they have worked so hard in life for your happiness could you explain your presence without achieving it?

They are not missing you. These types of emotions are reserved for the living.

Take all the time you need. You may feel like you are in a daze and have lost your purpose in life. It will take time to process and understand what has happened and decide how to move forward.

It may be difficult, but when you are ready, take a deep breath and refocus your thoughts on getting your life back on track.

Much like grief, there may come a time when you literally cannot go forward, you're done. Your mind is frayed, you feel confused and are mentally, even physically exhausted. You should never get to this point, but many people do.

You are burned out.

Burnout can happen to anyone. When burnout happens, self-care is essential. Don't wait until you've burned out to take a break.

Humans are fragile, delicate *and* powerful . . . like computer chips. You are made this way so that you can be flexible, reactive to the world around you and able to protect yourself. You can make quick decisions and make mental, emotional and physical U-turns. You can think on your feet. You are agile. But such flexibility can cause buckling and leave you fatigued and unlike computer chips, you will need rest to replenish your source of energy.

I once worked one scheduled 10-hour shift too many at your standard desk job, without proper rest. I was beyond exhausted and had reached my mental and physical limit. *Before* that workday began, I already knew one of two things was going to happen: I would either reach the end of my workday and try to make up for the rest that I had been putting off or I would pass out and die. Obviously, I survived that day, but it should never have happened. Minds can break. Bodies you can break. Even strong minds and strong bodies. Your mental, physical and emotional well-being must be paramount. If you lose your grip on any one of these, you could lose everything.

Interestingly, burnout can come over you without your realizing it. You choose to work through natural breaks or allow other responsibilities to fall by the wayside, all to get a project done. You may have taken on a bigger load than you can handle. You may feel yourself becoming less productive, but you do not attribute it to overwork. Then you reach a breaking point. It is hard to keep your thoughts organized and your enthusiasm and productivity hit a wall that is a heavy lift to get over.

Burnout does not always correlate with overwork. Maybe your life is moving at a faster pace than you can keep up with; you may feel like you're falling behind. Keeping up with your children's schedules, being overwhelmed by schoolwork or even household chores can trigger burnout.

One way to take care of yourself is by talking to someone close to you about your feelings. People who care about you will be there for you. If you're feeling overwhelmed and don't know what to do, try taking a break from your busy schedule and spending time with family or friends.

How to avoid burnout:

1. Review your schedule. Assess what must be tackled immediately, what

can wait and what does not need to be done at all.

2. Delegate. There's no need for you to take on every task. Whenever possible take the opportunity to delegate repetitive tasks, teachable tasks or tasks that can be better done by others.

3. Hire it out. Housework, minor repairs, grocery shopping and more, there are services available to do these chores and do them well. Take advantage of them when you feel overwhelmed.

4. Keep a Journal. Daily journaling can allow you to see when things are starting to go off the rails. Even missing journal entries when you normally journal consistently can be an early sign of burnout.

5. Create a to-do list.   Keep yourself organized with a to-do list.   By keeping track of your tasks, you can not only gauge what has been done and what needs to be done but *when* you can take your breaks without affecting workflow.

6. Take frequent breaks. Include short and extended breaks in your schedule. Whether it's a morning tea break, a quick nap, or a short walk, don't let breaks just happen organically. Plan for them and plan what you intend to do with them therefore, you truly experience your break as opposed to taking a break and not mentally or physically acknowledging that it happened.

Being able to step back allows you to come back stronger and more resilient. You may need to take a break from your daily routine, but have you ever taken time off and felt like it hadn't happened?

It is important to make sure you have a plan for the time you are taking off.

1. Schedule a day off to go to the spa while your children are at school.

2. Hire a babysitter and treat yourself to room service at a nice hotel.

3. Volunteer at a local animal shelter. You'll feel great knowing that you are helping an animal in need.

4. If you like to read, make a list of books that you want to read.

5. If you like to write, make a list of ideas for stories that you want to write.

6. Learn a new language and join a language meetup to practice your new skills.

7. If you enjoy sports, join a local sports club.

8. Join your local theater group for a creative outlet.

9. Join a knitting, walking or hiking group.

10. Do nothing, literally.

Do whatever you need to do to recapture your 'me' time.

THOUGHTS:

_____

_____

_____

_____

_____

_____

_____

_____

_____

_____

_____

_____

_____

_____

"The messier your life, the more you need to let go"

CHAPTER 10

DECLUTTER YOUR SPACE; DECLUTTER YOUR MIND

Regardless of what you are accustomed to, it is difficult to flourish in a messy environment.

It is important to create an environment that is conducive to success. This can be as simple as having a positive phrase on your desk or a motivational poster. Hang a beautiful painting on the wall or pictures of places you want to visit. Keep soft music or ambient sounds playing softly in the background, mood music isn't just for elevators. These things will help you to stay positive and motivated.

One of the most important factors in mental and emotional health is the environment you create. This includes what you see every day when you wake up, the space you work in and so on. Do you have to step over a pile of dirty laundry in the morning? Does your work desk double as a catch-all for dusty knickknacks that have no proper home? A positive mindset thrives in a positive environment. In order to create a positive environment, you must ensure that your surroundings are free from external stressors. You accomplish this by making sure your home is clean and clutter-free. You should also make sure that you have the right amount of space for you and your family.

Don't overlook aesthetics when it comes to creating a positive environment. When you come home after a hard day and your home is a mess and the breakfast dishes are still in the sink, it can feel discouraging.

If you are generally rushed in the morning, either load the dishwasher before you go or use paper plates and plastic utensils for easy clean-up. Get a small robot vacuum you can set to sweep up while you're out of the house. Open the curtains and allow natural light to sweep across the room, anything that makes you feel good or inspires you. Schedule a day to clean and organize your space. One day, one room. If possible, hire a maid service for the day to clean your home. This will give a baseline of cleanliness you can strive to maintain.

Make your life easier and set yourself up for success.

THOUGHTS:

_____

_____

_____

_____

_____

_____

_____

_____

_____

_____

_____

_____

_____

_____

_____

Declutter Your Space; Declutter Your Mind

_____

_____

_____

_____

_____

_____

_____

_____

_____

_____

_____

_____

_____

_____

_____

"Positivity makes you a magnet for positive experiences"

CHAPTER 11

WHAT POSITIVITY CAN DO

Do you want to be a magnet for positive experiences?

When you are in a good mood, your mind is at ease. Your thoughts are less cluttered, and you are more efficient at completing the tasks you set out for yourself.

A positive mindset can improve your mood, memory, creativity and productivity. It can also help you to be more motivated and make better decisions.

Being a positive person has a number of benefits. It can reduce stress and improve sleep. You will be more resilient and less prone to getting sick. It's never too late to change your outlook. These are all benefits of a positive mindset. It will lead you to a healthier, happier, more successful life.

Positivity and optimism are contagious and your state of mind will naturally carry over into everything you do.

This type of perspective is not only great for managing your own life, but for dealing with the people in your professional life. However, professionally you don't always get to pick and choose who you associate with. You may realize that everyone you come in contact with, whether it's because of poor people skills, a negative personality or they simply rub you the wrong way, may not support ongoing, stress-free interaction.

As you may need to interact with these people daily, you will need to take precautions. Instead of focusing on their negative aspects, focus only on why you need to interact with them and avoid all other unnecessary interactions that may cause you stress.

Being positive will help you build stronger relationships, make new friends and have a better social life. It is important to foster positivity in your personal relationships. People seek out positive people and interactions to counteract the negativity in their own lives.

Adopting a positive mindset will make you more productive and energetic as your attitude towards life is an important factor in achieving your goals. It can also keep you healthy as your new found energy can be poured into more activities and exercise.

Another benefit is not having to worry about things not going according to plan because you now have the confidence to know that you can handle whatever life throws at you.

A positive outlook allows you to give others the benefit of the doubt. Many people spend their lives reliving various slights and offenses determined that the world is against them. No one is perfect. People don't always get it right the first time, including in their interactions with you.   Not every slight is purposeful or meant as an offense.

Consequently, every off-hand remark or careless gesture is not a reason to become offended. Most people will not set out to hurt you with an off-hand joke or remark. They are more likely to believe it to be funny or insightful and based on their prior encounters or experiences within their circle of friends, assumed that you too would find it amusing or clever.

Do not confuse this with having a different outlook on hot-button issues.

There is a common saying that you do not talk about politics or religion. These can be volatile issues to discuss in unfamiliar social settings. However, if you find yourself in a social setting where the conversation has turned towards politics or religion, you have two options.

First, walk away. While the conversation may start off engaging and interesting, it could quickly turn south. Therefore, your first, best option would be to discreetly *walk away.*

Your second option would be to attempt to turn the conversation back to more appropriate social discourse. If you don't have the confidence in your skills at pulling this off, go for option number one.

These issues involve long, heart-felt beliefs and everyone has a right to their personal opinions. Opposing opinions will not be consolidated over lunch.

You talk how you talk and usually try to act according to your best behavior, especially when meeting new people. How you interact with the world is based on your prior interactions. Your successful interactions, the ones that have yielded friendships and positive associations in the past, teach you what works and what doesn't. However, prior interactions do not always translate well to every encounter.

When that happens, what happens next can best be described as a 'social disconnect' rather than an intentional offense.

In social situations, people generally want to be liked, they want to be thought of as witty or congenial, they want to make friends. Their attempt to do so may not always be successful, but at least they are making an attempt. You have the power to guide them in the right direction and salvage an awkward introduction or encounter with someone who is at least willing to try. You also have the power to take offense and assume they hold some personal animosity towards you.

Of course, there are people in the world who are truly offensive and unsalvageable. These people have usually managed to ignore the cues from prior interactions and are probably distasteful to not only your sensibilities but to others as well. Encounters with these kinds of people are most likely to be few and far between and certainly not worth ruining your day or your sense of peace to be offended when you can simply smile and walk away.

When some people get shut down, rudely dismissed, or labeled as offensive because of an awkward interaction, they usually stop trying, and what benefit is that to the world?

It is important to give people the same benefit of the doubt that you would like afforded to you in the same or similar circumstances.

Positivity allows you the freedom to not feel the need to compare yourself to others. Everyone is on their own journey and no one will have the same experience as you. There are many ways to reach the same destination.

When you forge your own path you can focus on what matters to you and filter out what doesn't. You can assess your progress by your own standards and not by arbitrary benchmarks set by others.

Be confident in who you are and enjoy the ride!

Positivity is a form of energy that attracts good things and naturally leads to happiness. Here are some ways to become more positive about your life:

- Be grateful for what you have.

- Focus on the present.

- Don't compare yourself to others.

- Give your time to others.

- Be optimistic.

- Be kind.

- Give others the benefit of the doubt.

Points to Remember:

1. Positive thinking can help you achieve your goals. When you stop worrying about the future and focus on the present, you will be able to achieve your goals.

2. It makes you feel good. When you are positive, you will have more energy, more motivation, and more enthusiasm.

3. It helps you live a healthier life. When you are positive, you will be less likely to become depressed and develop illnesses such as high blood pressure, high cholesterol, and heart disease.

4. It helps you become more successful. When you are positive, you will be able to get more things done and have more energy.

5. It helps you become more self-aware. When you are positive, you will be able to see your mistakes and own them.

6. It helps you become more patient. When you are positive, you will be less likely to get frustrated and make rash decisions.

Positivity is like a muscle, the more you exercise it the stronger it becomes. You will become adept at employing it at the best of times and in the most difficult circumstances. It will help you stay balanced, grounded and productive. Positivity will keep you focused on the path that leads to happiness.

THOUGHTS:

_____

_____

_____

_____

_____

_____

_____

_____

_____

_____

_____

_____

_____

_____

_____

_____

_____

_____

_____

_____

_____

_____

_____

_____

_____

_____

_____

_____

_____

_____

_____

"Life moves in one direction.
You can't change the past"

CHAPTER 12

POSITIVITY AND THE WORLD AROUND YOU

The more positive you are, the more people around you will respond in kind. You will find that people around you will be more caring, helpful and understanding. Be consistent. Inconsistent behavior breeds suspicion.

This is not to discount the subset of people who have chosen to wallow in misery or people who, for whatever reason, just don't like you. They'll have to wade through their own struggles and their own negativity, but that has nothing to do with you.

Your attitude can either make or break someone's day. When you are steeped in negativity, the corresponding response from people around you will be palpable. When you are positive, people are going to be drawn to you.

While you are on your journey to a more positive you, give others the benefit of the doubt. Have the grace to acknowledge that they may have not yet begun their journey. Positively or negatively, you should always be aware of how your attitude affects others. Everyone has good days and bad days and it's easy to get caught up in your thoughts and forget that others may be struggling too.

In the end, what you put out into the world will come back to you.

THOUGHTS:

_____

_____

_____

_____

_____

_____

_____

_____

_____

_____

_____

_____

_____

_____

"Life is a lot easier to manage in smaller pieces"

CHAPTER 13

SMALL STEPS; BIG CHANGES

Life is a lot easier to manage in smaller pieces.

When you feel overwhelmed, set small, intermediate goals that are achievable and rewarding. You will acquire a sense of accomplishment and confidence that can be easily transferred to larger goals.

For example, if you want to lose weight, you could start by taking the stairs instead of the elevator for one flight. Gradually, you can work your way up to walking up three flights of stairs. You could set aside one day to clean one room instead of the whole house. Designate three days of the week in which you'll make the bed in the morning and work up to making it a daily routine. When you break down tedious chores into smaller pieces, you inadvertently reduce stress.

Stress is a major cause of fear, anxiety, and negativity.

Instead of addressing the stress triggers in your life, you may be getting by using negative coping mechanisms. Negative coping mechanisms are ways of coping with stress that end up having negative effects on your mental or physical health.

For example, if you are feeling overwhelmed, you may find yourself reaching for a glass of alcohol. This is a negative coping mechanism because it may temporarily relieve your stress but can also lead to other problems. These other problems may include an increase in anxiety, a decrease in focus, and an increase in depression. So instead of using negative coping mechanisms, it is important to identify your stressors, tackle them head-on and find ways of coping with stress without these ineffective mechanisms. They resolve nothing and instead will set back or stall your progress.

Once you recognize that you have been using negative coping mechanisms to deal with stress, zero in on when the urge to engage them materializes. What are you thinking about? Is it something that has been on your mind all day? All week? Did you just receive news that triggered you? By now, your coping mechanisms have become habitual, so you will need to slow down and pay special attention to weed them out.

If you're ready to leave negativity behind and commit to a life in harmony with your true self, let your stress triggers guide you.

Write down your thoughts and feelings about your day, about your life, about the people in your life. Write about your goals and ambitions and how you propose to achieve them. Then, put it away for a few days. When you come back to it, observe how many of your thoughts and feelings were negative. You may even realize that some of your assessments are not true or helpful.

Avoid small stressors.

Have you ever been in a hurry and just as you're about to leave the house you realize that you can't find your keys? You're already running late and you can feel the frustration building and the stress rising in your body. Prepare a place for your keys and make a habit of leaving your keys there whenever you come home.

Does your hair stand on end every time the phone rings because of your history with telemarketers or bill collectors? Try placing your phone on silent and letting your callers leave a message, then you can decide which calls to return and which to ignore.

These are one of the many small stressors in life that can easily be avoided or alleviated.

Pay attention to persistent stressors.

When you walk into your place of employment do you feel like a refrigerator is about to land on your head? It could be your boss, a co-worker or the job itself that is triggering you. The job may just not be the right fit for you. You may have a position that requires you to talk to people on the phone or make cold calls. If the thought of picking up the phone to speak to someone new or even regular clients causes you stress, or if deadlines cause you to break out in a rash, then, while you are employed, start looking for a new job, one in line with how you are most productive and who you truly are.

Challenge your stressors.

From now on as you go through your day, look for your small stress triggers, look for your large stress triggers, no longer will you ignore them. Weed out your stressors and address them one by one.

Points to Remember:

1. Break down overwhelming tasks into smaller pieces.

2. Stop using negative coping mechanisms.

3. Do not ignore stress triggers.

4. Challenge your stress triggers head-on.

5. Address your stress triggers one by one.

THOUGHTS:

_____

_____

_____

_____

_____

_____

_____

_____

_____

_____

_____

_____

_____

_____

How to Stay Positive Without Losing Your Mind!

"Be grateful for small blessings"

CHAPTER 14

PRACTICE GRATITUDE

It's important to be honest about your feelings and not just put on a happy face. However, there is also something to be said about being grateful, even for the smallest blessings.

It is easy to get caught up in the stress of everyday life and forget about the little things that make life worth living. Remember to be grateful for what you have and acknowledge the positive things that exist in your life. They are easily overlooked. Take time out of your day to relax and, as they say, 'smell the roses.'

No matter how bad things get, there is always something to be grateful for. It is not always easy to be thankful, but, in truth, there are always good things happening around you, even when you're too preoccupied to notice.

Gratitude helps you to appreciate the blessings in even the smallest things or the small kindnesses that have been shown to you. When you are feeling down and hopeless, it can help you feel better. Appreciating the little things in life is something that many people forget to do. You may not recognize it at the present moment, but even the smallest blessings can make a huge difference in your life.

Everyone has something to be thankful for. It is easy to forget how lucky you are to have food to eat, clean water to drink, shelter, and family. If you have some or even none of these things at the moment, are you healthy? Some people are struggling with their health. Do you have someone to talk to? Many people are struggling with loneliness. Are you able to provide for yourself and your family? Many lives are being challenged by low or no employment. Wherever you are on the spectrum of life's challenges, know that others have faced the same or worse challenges.

As it has been said, '. . . there is no new thing under the sun' (Ecclesiastes 1:9). These and many more challenges have been faced and conquered before. They have been conquered by people who aren't as gifted as you, people who aren't as persistent as you, people who don't have a quarter of the advantages as you.

Every day, take time to reflect on the advantages you have, what you have accomplished (no matter how small) and what you are grateful for. Being grateful for the smallest blessings helps you appreciate the bigger things in life and opens the door to more blessings.

Gratitude is a 'thank you' to God and your Universe. Thank you for even the smallest blessing and thank you for the blessings to come. It is a bit like gathering flowers. As you gather the flowers that appeal to you, you smell them, appreciate them and look around confidently for more.

Here are some ways you can practice gratitude:

1. Create a list of things you're grateful for and keep it with you.

2. Write down 3 things that happened during the day, whether it be an experience, a person, or a place, that made you feel grateful.

3. Set a reminder on your phone or calendar to remind yourself to think about something that you are grateful for.

4. Spend time with someone you are grateful to have in your life.

In difficult times or when your mind becomes cluttered by the events of the day, you will forget the beauty of sunsets or many of the things that once brought you joy and peace.   This is why you must practice gratitude. You must make it a habit.

In the bible, Luke 17:11-19 tells the story of when Jesus healed ten lepers of a certain village. He sent them off to show themselves to the priests of the village and there was only one who returned to say 'thank you.' Be that one.

THOUGHTS:

_____

_____

_____

_____

_____

_____

_____

_____

_____

_____

_____

_____

_____

_____

_____

_____

_____

_____

_____

_____

_____

_____

_____

_____

_____

_____

_____

_____

_____

_____

_____

"Perfect is not necessary"

CHAPTER 15

A PRACTICAL GUIDE

1.   What are your negative coping mechanisms?

_____

_____

_____

_____

_____

_____

_____

_____

_____

_____

_____

2.   Make a list of your stressors [large and small].

_____

_____

_____

_____

_____

_____

_____

_____

_____

_____

_____

_____

3.   How do you plan to challenge them?

_____

_____

_____

_____

_____

_____

_____

_____

_____

_____

_____

_____

_____

_____

4.   Have you experienced righteous negativity? Why?

_____

_____

_____

_____

_____

_____

_____

_____

_____

_____

_____

_____

_____

_____

5.　　　Are you ready to let it go?

---

6.   What positive affirmations would you like to incorporate into your daily routine?

_____

_____

_____

_____

_____

_____

_____

_____

_____

_____

_____

_____

_____

7.   List 3 things you can change about your living space to make it more visually appealing.

_____

_____

_____

_____

_____

_____

_____

_____

_____

_____

_____

_____

8.   List 3 or more steps you plan to take to treat yourself better.

_____

_____

_____

_____

_____

_____

_____

_____

_____

_____

_____

_____

_____

9.   What are you grateful for?

_____

_____

_____

_____

_____

_____

_____

_____

_____

_____

_____

_____

_____

_____

THOUGHTS:

_____

_____

_____

_____

_____

_____

_____

_____

_____

_____

_____

_____

_____

_____

_____

_____

_____

_____

_____

_____

_____

_____

_____

_____

_____

_____

_____

_____

_____

_____

"Release the resentments of the past and focus on the possibilities of the future"

CHAPTER 16

FINAL THOUGHTS

Negative thinking is dangerous. It does not matter where it comes from or how it began, how you were raised or who is to blame. You will now live in the present moment. You will now take control of your life. You will now accept responsibility for your future.

This is the first step in a new journey, one where you are determined to make positive changes in your life and it starts with a commitment to moving forward, positively. I want to help you by providing you with this guide to start living your life with confidence!

THOUGHTS:

_____

_____

_____

_____

_____

_____

_____

_____

_____

_____

_____

_____

_____

_____

_____

_____

_____

_____

_____

_____

_____

_____

_____

_____

_____

_____

_____

_____

_____

_____

You May Also Like:

Cocktails and Crayons Adult Coloring Books
Volumes I - VI

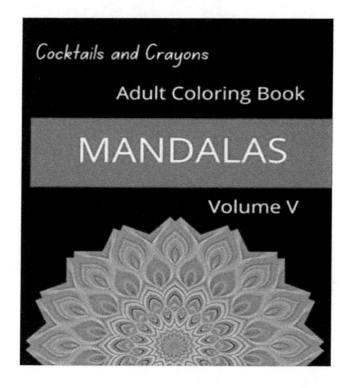

Available at:
https://www.amazon.com/author/genesisbooks

Enjoy the creative therapy of coloring with these adult coloring books. A fun therapeutic way to relax, focus and relieve stress.

CPSIA information can be obtained
at www.ICGtesting.com
Printed in the USA
LVHW050002160523
747099LV00017B/1256